Quilter's DESK DIARY 2014

Welcome to 2014

Stay organized in style with *The Quilter's Desk Diary 2014*. Illustrated throughout with beautiful photographs of inspirational quilts from the most talented of quiltmakers, each week-to-view diary page has plenty of room for your own personal notes. If you want to find out more about any of the quiltmakers featured, turn to the back of the book for information about them and the books they have written.

D&C
David and Charles
www.stitchcraftcreate.co.uk

30
Monday

31
Tuesday

New Years Day

1
Wednesday 2025

2
Thursday

3
Friday

4
Saturday

5
Sunday

JANUARY						
M	T	W	T	F	S	S
		1	2	3	4	5
6	7	8	9	10	11	12
13	14	15	16	17	18	19
20	21	22	23	24	25	26
27	28	29	30	31		

Here and There
Make a New Year's resolution to introduce a younger member of your family to quilting. There is no better place to start them off than with Elizabeth Betts' *Beginner's Guide to Quilting*. It features 16 fresh, contemporary designs, including this stylish lap quilt, all specially designed to introduce the basic concepts of the craft.

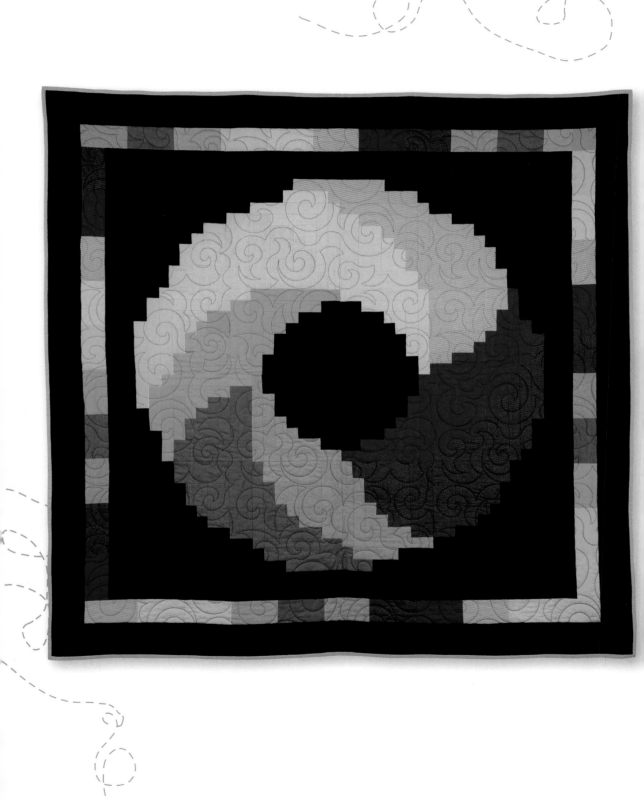

6
Monday

7
Tuesday

8
Wednesday

9
Thursday

10
Friday

11
Saturday

12
Sunday

Black Hole

Brenda Sanders had only been quilting for two years when she decided to take the plunge and enter Pam and Nicky Lintott's Jelly Roll Dream Challenge competition. Entrants had to make their quilt designs using just one Jelly Roll™. The competition attracted contributions from all over the world and the winning quilt designs – including Brenda's – can be seen in *Jelly Roll Dreams*.

			JANUARY			
M	T	W	T	F	S	S
		1	2	3	4	5
6	7	8	9	10	11	12
13	14	15	16	17	18	19
20	21	22	23	24	25	26
27	28	29	30	31		

January

13
Monday

14
Tuesday

15
Wednesday

16
Thursday

17
Friday

18
Saturday

19
Sunday

Strolling Garden

The *tsukiyama* bed quilt features in *Easy Japanese Quilt Style* by Julia Davis and Anne Muxworthy, a collection of 10 stylish but simple projects inspired by Japanese fabric. *Tsukiyama* translates as 'strolling garden' and the easy piece blocks are the flower beds while the green sashing is the path that meanders around the garden. This design successfully combines large pattern and small print fabrics.

JANUARY

M	T	W	T	F	S	S
		1	2	3	4	5
6	7	8	9	10	11	12
13	14	15	16	17	18	19
20	21	22	23	24	25	26
27	28	29	30	31		

January

Martin Luther King Day (US)

20
Monday

21
Tuesday

22
Wednesday

23
Thursday

24
Friday

25
Saturday

Australia Day (Aus)

26
Sunday

Heirloom Sampler

Make this the year you make the heirloom quilt you have always promised yourself. You will find plenty of inspiration for choosing your blocks from the 40 featured in Lynne Edwards' *The Essential Sampler Quilt Book*, which provides masterclass instruction for making a sampler quilt just like this one made by Collie Parker.

JANUARY

M	T	W	T	F	S	S
		1	2	3	4	5
6	7	8	9	10	11	12
13	14	15	16	17	18	19
20	21	22	23	24	25	26
27	28	29	30	31		

January/February

27
Monday

28
Tuesday

29
Wednesday

30
Thursday

Chinese New Year

31
Friday

1
Saturday

2
Sunday

Summer Skies Pincushion

These bright little pincushions show off the elegant curve of Cathedral Window to great effect. They were designed by Lynne Edwards as the perfect starter project for this classic folded technique which is explored in detail in her book *Cathedral Window Quilts*.

			JANUARY			
M	T	W	T	F	S	S
		1	2	3	4	5
6	7	8	9	10	11	12
13	14	15	16	17	18	19
20	21	22	23	24	25	26
27	28	29	30	31		

February

3
Monday

4
Tuesday

5
Wednesday

6
Thursday

7
Friday

8
Saturday

9
Sunday

Chain Reaction

In *Antique to Heirloom Jelly Roll Quilts*, Pam and Nicky Lintott bring you 12 Jelly Roll™ quilt designs based on the best antique quilts in Pam's stunning collection of vintage quilts. This one is based on a 1930s American quilt with a triple Irish Chain layout. While honouring the original's design layout, they have chosen very vibrant colours and extrovert patterns for their modern classic.

FEBRUARY

M	T	W	T	F	S	S
					1	2
3	4	5	6	7	8	9
10	11	12	13	14	15	16
17	18	19	20	21	22	23
24	25	26	27	28		

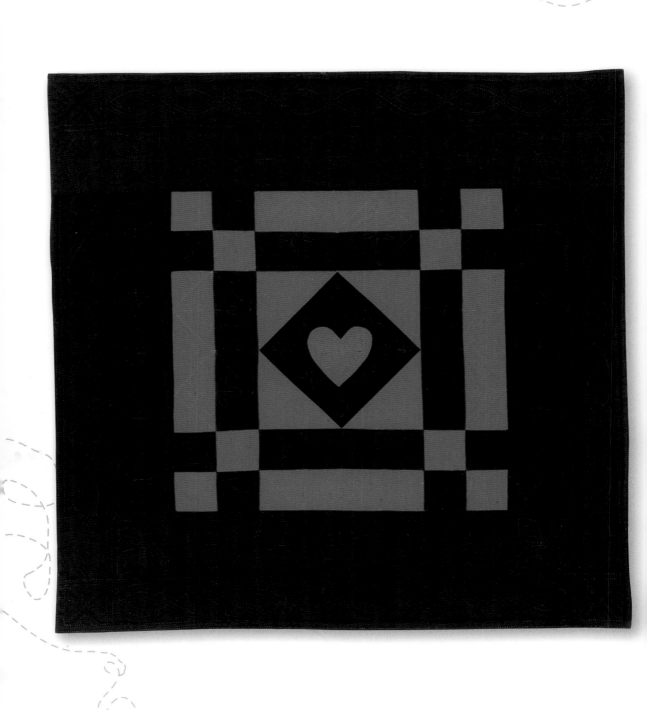

10
Monday

11
Tuesday

12
Wednesday

13
Thursday

Valentine's Day

14
Friday

15
Saturday

16
Sunday

Cariad Quilt II

Making Welsh Quilts by Mary Jenkins and Clare Claridge explores the history of traditional Welsh quilting. The inspiration for this piece was a very large wool quilt from Pembrokeshire, and Clare Claridge has made a small replica of it using red and black cotton fabrics. Cariad is Welsh for 'sweetheart' and the heart was a popular motif often seen on Welsh quilts.

			FEBRUARY			
M	T	W	T	F	S	S
					1	2
3	4	5	6	7	8	9
10	11	12	13	14	15	16
17	18	19	20	21	22	23
24	25	26	27	28		

February

17
Monday

18
Tuesday

19
Wednesday

20
Thursday

21
Friday

22
Saturday

23
Sunday

A Sense of Direction

Mary Claire Allen's very first Jelly Roll™ quilt was a real winner.
She entered it in the 2011 Jelly Roll Dream Challenge and judges
Pam and Nicky Lintott chose it as one of the 12 winning entries. Her
design was inspired by the traditional Flying Geese quilt patterns
she had seen in quilt books belonging to her mother, and she wanted
to capture the same feeling of movement in a fresh new way.

FEBRUARY

M	T	W	T	F	S	S
					1	2
3	4	5	6	7	8	9
10	11	12	13	14	15	16
17	18	19	20	21	22	23
24	25	26	27	28		

24
Monday

25
Tuesday

26
Wednesday

27
Thursday

28
Friday

1
Saturday

2
Sunday

Pink Paradise Birdsong

Susan Briscoe's quilt design was awarded first place in the category of Quilt Art at the Great Northern Quilt Show, and it is a great reminder that sashiko doesn't have to be restricted to Japanese theme projects. However, if you do prefer to work your sashiko more traditionally, you will find plenty of inspiration in Susan's book, *Japanese Sashiko Inspirations*.

		FEBRUARY				
M	T	W	T	F	S	S
					1	2
3	4	5	6	7	8	9
10	11	12	13	14	15	16
17	18	19	20	21	22	23
24	25	26	27	28		

3
Monday

Shrove Tuesday

4
Tuesday

5
Wednesday

6
Thursday

7
Friday

8
Saturday

9
Sunday

Galaxy

Charm square packs are a quick way to make a quilt. When you choose fabric you love you can just sew the squares together at random and you will end up with a lovely looking quilt. With just a little bit of extra work you can make this absolutely gorgeous quilt (featured in Pam and Nicky Lintott's *More Layer Cake, Jelly Roll & Charm Quilts*) which looks far more complex than it really is.

			MARCH			
M	T	W	T	F	S	S
					1	2
3	4	5	6	7	8	9
10	11	12	13	14	15	16
17	18	19	20	21	22	23
24	25	26	27	28	29	30
31						

March

10
Monday

11
Tuesday

12
Wednesday

13
Thursday

14
Friday

15
Saturday

16
Sunday

Temples and Fans

Bring the simplicity and sophistication of Japanese style into your home with the easy-to-make quilt collection featured in Susan Briscoe's *Japanese Quilt Inspirations*. The sensu (fan) quilt features a 20cm (8in) fan block which is easy to make using machine sewn freezer appliqué, and sashiko-style big stitch, hand-stitched with red thread, echoes the fan outlines.

MARCH

M	T	W	T	F	S	S
					1	2
3	4	5	6	7	8	9
10	11	12	13	14	15	16
17	18	19	20	21	22	23
24	25	26	27	28	29	30
31						

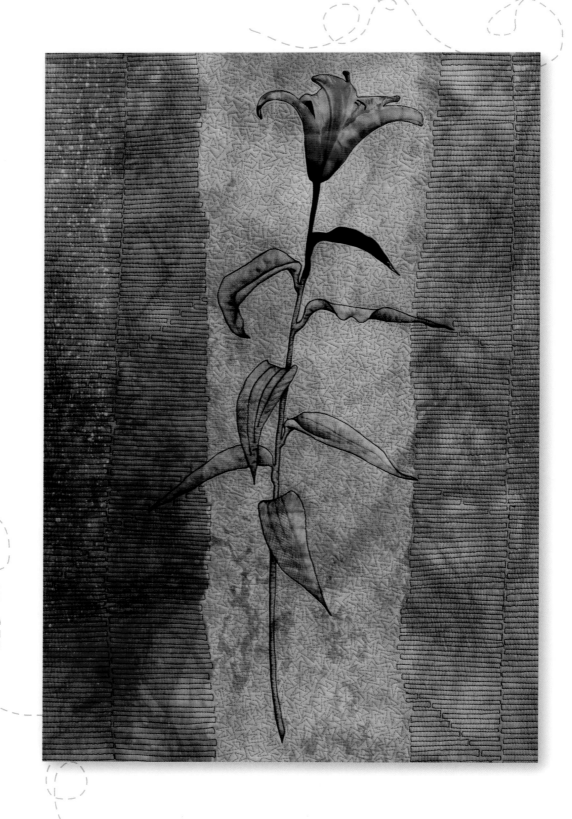

17
Monday

18
Tuesday

19
Wednesday

20
Thursday

21
Friday

22
Saturday

23
Sunday

Blue Lily

If you are ready to explore your creative side *The Painted Quilt* by Linda and Laura Kemshall will offer plenty of inspiration as you find your own style. This photograph shows a detail from one of Laura's quilts which features an ink-jet transfer using heat transfer paper. A pale, vertical band was bleached through the centre and finally details of leaves and stems were drawn with pen.

		MARCH				
M	T	W	T	F	S	S
					1	2
3	4	5	6	7	8	9
10	11	12	13	14	15	16
17	18	19	20	21	22	23
24	25	26	27	28	29	30
31						

24
Monday

25
Tuesday

26
Wednesday

27
Thursday

28
Friday

29
Saturday

Mother's Day (UK)

30
Sunday

Little Hexagons

Making a smaller project is an ideal way to try out a new technique. This gorgeous little doll's quilt, from Helen Philipps' *Pretty Patchwork Gifts*, is made using the English paper piecing technique – it's simple and fun but the results are impressive. Helen's book is full of beautiful projects made in fresh, contemporary fabrics that are ideal for giving.

MARCH						
M	T	W	T	F	S	S
					1	2
3	4	5	6	7	8	9
10	11	12	13	14	15	16
17	18	19	20	21	22	23
24	25	26	27	28	29	30
31						

31
Monday

1
Tuesday

2
Wednesday

3
Thursday

4
Friday

5
Saturday

6
Sunday

Silver Blue Tower

In this wall hanging Lynne Edwards has created a shimmering tower of Cathedral Window squares and set it against a 'sky' of Secret Garden folded background squares. As she has chosen to make it from a grey/blue palette of shimmering silk, her piece evokes the glistening puddles left after all those April showers. Lynne's book *Cathedral Window Quilts* provides a wealth of inspiration for exploring this classic folded technique.

APRIL

M	T	W	T	F	S	S
	1	2	3	4	5	6
7	8	9	10	11	12	13
14	15	16	17	18	19	20
21	22	23	24	25	26	27
28	29	30				

April

7
Monday

8
Tuesday

9
Wednesday

10
Thursday

11
Friday

12
Saturday

13
Sunday

Woven Baskets

In *Folk Quilt Appliqué* Clare Kingslake shares her appliqué secrets to make over 20 irresistible projects inspired by folk art. To create the sweet little basket on this wall hanging for example, she has used strips of fabric to represent the basket weave, intertwining them as she appliqués them to the background fabric. You can have great fun mixing pretty fabrics to make baskets of different colours.

APRIL

M	T	W	T	F	S	S
	1	2	3	4	5	6
7	8	9	10	11	12	13
14	15	16	17	18	19	20
21	22	23	24	25	26	27
28	29	30				

14
Monday

15
Tuesday

16
Wednesday

17
Thursday

Good Friday (UK, Aus)

18
Friday

19
Saturday

Easter Sunday

20
Sunday

Hen Party

Dessert Rolls™ are the latest delicious bundle of pre-cut fabrics available from Moda. Each perfectly coordinated collection of 20 5in-strips cut across the width of the fabric can produce a stunning quilt top when working the designs featured in Pam and Nicky Lintott's latest book, *Dessert Roll Quilts*. Hen Party is just one of 12 gorgeous new quilt designs they have specially created to inspire you to try out this exciting new fabric concept.

APRIL

M	T	W	T	F	S	S
	1	2	3	4	5	6
7	8	9	10	11	12	13
14	15	16	17	18	19	20
21	22	23	24	25	26	27
28	29	30				

April

Easter Monday (UK, Aus)

21
Monday

22
Tuesday

23
Wednesday

24
Thursday

25
Friday

26
Saturday

27
Sunday

Red and White Basket

The Quilters' Guild Heritage Collection has more than 700 pieces to inspire today's quilting generation. Sometimes very little is known about the quiltmakers but each quilt provides a tantalizing clue to its origins. The basket block was typical of British quilts of the late 19th century and the blue pencil used to mark the detailed hand quilting was a popular transfer method with North Country quilters. More historic quilts can be seen in *The Quilters' Guild Collection*.

APRIL

M	T	W	T	F	S	S
	1	2	3	4	5	6
7	8	9	10	11	12	13
14	15	16	17	18	19	20
21	22	23	24	25	26	27
28	29	30				

28
Monday

29
Tuesday

30
Wednesday

1
Thursday

2
Friday

3
Saturday

4
Sunday

Shadow Appliqué Rose

With over 220 patchwork, appliqué and quilting techniques featured, *The Quilter's Bible* by Linda Clements is the essential resource for every quilter's library. There are so many exciting and creative skills to explore including beautifully delicate shadow appliqué, which has been used here to decorate a simple drawstring bag with a Mackintosh-style rose design.

APRIL						
M	T	W	T	F	S	S
	1	2	3	4	5	6
7	8	9	10	11	12	13
14	15	16	17	18	19	20
21	22	23	24	25	26	27
28	29	30				

May

Bank Holiday (UK)

5
Monday

6
Tuesday

7
Wednesday

8
Thursday

9
Friday

10
Saturday

Mother's Day (US, Aus)

11
Sunday

Feathered Star

Marsha McCloskey's fascination with Feathered Star blocks began over 30 years ago, and in that time she has collected and recorded hundreds of variations. The larger the star, the larger the centre square or octagon, giving more opportunity for you to add piecing as can be seen in this wall hanging. Marsha's Feathered Star masterclass can be found in *The Quiltmakers*.

MAY

M	T	W	T	F	S	S
			1	2	3	4
5	6	7	8	9	10	11
12	13	14	15	16	17	18
19	20	21	22	23	24	25
26	27	28	29	30	31	

12
Monday

13
Tuesday

14
Wednesday

15
Thursday

16
Friday

17
Saturday

18
Sunday

North by Northwest

Pam and Nicky Lintott have used an Antique Fair Jelly Roll™ by Blackbeard Designs to faithfully recreate the lovely colours of their original inspiration, an American 19th century sawtooth quilt from Pam's vintage quilt collection. This is just one of 12 new Jelly Roll™ designs featured in *Antique to Heirloom Jelly Roll Quilts*.

			MAY			
M	T	W	T	F	S	S
			1	2	3	4
5	6	7	8	9	10	11
12	13	14	15	16	17	18
19	20	21	22	23	24	25
26	27	28	29	30	31	

19
Monday

20
Tuesday

21
Wednesday

22
Thursday

23
Friday

24
Saturday

25
Sunday

Welsh Wool

The Quilters' Guild Heritage Collection is an incredible testament to over 400 years of the best of British quilt making and some of the best pieces in the collection can be seen in *The Quilters' Guild Collection*. This Welsh wool quilt, thought to have been made by Mrs Megan Jones at the end of the 19th or the beginning of the 20th century, is a typical example of Welsh quilts of the period.

				MAY		
M	T	W	T	F	S	S
			1	2	3	4
5	6	7	8	9	10	11
12	13	14	15	16	17	18
19	20	21	22	23	24	25
26	27	28	29	30	31	

Memorial Day (US)
Spring Bank Holiday (UK)

26
Monday

27
Tuesday

28
Wednesday

29
Thursday

30
Friday

31
Saturday

1
Sunday

Daisy Chain

Blanket Stitch Quilts by Lynne Edwards features 12 stunning projects for simple stick-and-stitch appliqué. When a repeat appliqué design is used in a quilt it can lose some of its impact if used on every single block, so here the daisy design is alternated with a Four-Patch/Nine-Patch combination block for an Irish Chain effect that frames and separates the daisy blocks beautifully.

			MAY			
M	T	W	T	F	S	S
			1	2	3	4
5	6	7	8	9	10	11
12	13	14	15	16	17	18
19	20	21	22	23	24	25
26	27	28	29	30	31	

2
Monday

3
Tuesday

4
Wednesday

5
Thursday

6
Friday

7
Saturday

8
Sunday

Rhubarb and Custard

In *Jelly Roll Sampler Quilts*, Pam and Nicky Lintott present a collection of over 50 patchwork block designs that you can pick-and-mix to make any number of quilt designs. For the Rhubarb and Custard quilt design three different blocks were used – King's Crown, Fox and Geese, and Shaded Trail – to make a stunning quilt using just one bright marble Jelly Roll™ from Moda.

			JUNE			
M	T	W	T	F	S	S
						1
2	3	4	5	6	7	8
9	10	11	12	13	14	15
16	17	18	19	20	21	22
23	24	25	26	27	28	29
30						

9
Monday

10
Tuesday

11
Wednesday

12
Thursday

13
Friday

14
Saturday

Father's Day (US, UK)

15
Sunday

Pennsylvania Echo

This simple little quilt, machine pieced and hand quilted by Clare Claridge in *Making Welsh Quilts*, is a replica of an early Welsh quilt found in America. The strong graphic design and subtle dark colours give it an Amish look although it pre-dates the earliest known Amish quilts by more than 50 years.

			JUNE			
M	T	W	T	F	S	S
						1
2	3	4	5	6	7	8
9	10	11	12	13	14	15
16	17	18	19	20	21	22
23	24	25	26	27	28	29
30						

16
Monday

17
Tuesday

18
Wednesday

19
Thursday

20
Friday

21
Saturday

22
Sunday

Pie Crust Cushion

Set in the heart of the Cornish countryside, Cowslip Workshops has to be the most tranquil of places to enjoy a quilting class. Set on an organic farm, it is run by Jo Colwill, who is constantly inspired by the countryside around her to create her beautiful cushions and quilts. She has collected her favourite designs together to share with you in *Cushions & Quilts*.

			JUNE			
M	T	W	T	F	S	S
						1
2	3	4	5	6	7	8
9	10	11	12	13	14	15
16	17	18	19	20	21	22
23	24	25	26	27	28	29
30						

23
Monday

24
Tuesday

25
Wednesday

26
Thursday

27
Friday

28
Saturday

29
Sunday

Tree of Life

The unknown needlewoman who made this early 19th century coverlet, featured in *The Quilters' Guild Collection*, has produced a stunning example of Broderie Perse, which literally translates as Persian embroidery. This appliqué method uses whole motifs of flowers, leaves, trees, birds and animals cut from printed fabrics and applied to a plain fabric to create a new design.

JUNE						
M	T	W	T	F	S	S
						1
2	3	4	5	6	7	8
9	10	11	12	13	14	15
16	17	18	19	20	21	22
23	24	25	26	27	28	29
30						

30
Monday

1
Tuesday

2
Wednesday

3
Thursday

Independence Day (US)

4
Friday

5
Saturday

6
Sunday

Sunken Hearth

The patchwork block on this quilt design is inspired by the *irori*, or sunken hearth, that used to be the centre of family life in traditional Japanese farmhouses. All the quilts featured in Susan Briscoe's *Japanese Quilt Inspirations* have been based on traditional Japanese motifs to allow you to present your Japanese fabrics in an authentic style.

			JULY			
M	T	W	T	F	S	S
	1	2	3	4	5	6
7	8	9	10	11	12	13
14	15	16	17	18	19	20
21	22	23	24	25	26	27
28	29	30	31			

7
Monday

8
Tuesday

9
Wednesday

10
Thursday

11
Friday

12
Saturday

13
Sunday

Cat's Cradle

Tessellating patterns – identical units that interlock with one another – are a great resource for quilters as Christine Porter discovers in *Tessellation Quilts*. Her starting point here was the hexagon shape, but when drafting it out she realized that she could create stars within the design by making separate hexagons and surrounding them with one colour – the red fabric for the inner stars.

			JULY			
M	T	W	T	F	S	S
	1	2	3	4	5	6
7	8	9	10	11	12	13
14	15	16	17	18	19	20
21	22	23	24	25	26	27
28	29	30	31			

14
Monday

15
Tuesday

16
Wednesday

17
Thursday

18
Friday

19
Saturday

20
Sunday

Building Blocks and Sherbet Lemon

In *Two From One Jelly Roll Quilts* Pam and Nicky Lintott show how to use just one Jelly Roll™ to make two quilts – half the fabric, but twice the inspiration. Here pastel fabrics were chosen to make two quick and easy cot quilts – the perfect gift for new parents.

JULY						
M	T	W	T	F	S	S
	1	2	3	4	5	6
7	8	9	10	11	12	13
14	15	16	17	18	19	20
21	22	23	24	25	26	27
28	29	30	31			

21
Monday

22
Tuesday

23
Wednesday

24
Thursday

25
Friday

26
Saturday

27
Sunday

Elephant Parade

This exotic wall hanging is just one of 12 appliqué projects featured in *Blanket Stitch Quilts* by Lynne Edwards. Alternating rows of elephant appliqués parade across three wide strips of background fabric, separated and framed with a narrow strip of contrast fabric. The finished design is bordered with an appliqué triangle design in the style of traditional Indian textiles.

			JULY			
M	T	W	T	F	S	S
	1	2	3	4	5	6
7	8	9	10	11	12	13
14	15	16	17	18	19	20
21	22	23	24	25	26	27
28	29	30	31			

28
Monday

29
Tuesday

30
Wednesday

31
Thursday

1
Friday

2
Saturday

3
Sunday

Cornish Wave

Cornish-based designer Jo Colwill was inspired by local sea views to create this cushion. It has a fresh, nautical feel, with its blue striped ticking and bright red boat sails and it is a great way to make use of old denim jeans. This is just one of 14 cushion designs featured in her book *Cushions & Quilts*, which also has six great quilt designs for you to choose from.

			JULY			
M	T	W	T	F	S	S
	1	2	3	4	5	6
7	8	9	10	11	12	13
14	15	16	17	18	19	20
21	22	23	24	25	26	27
28	29	30	31			

August

4
Monday

5
Tuesday

6
Wednesday

7
Thursday

8
Friday

9
Saturday

10
Sunday

Summer Fruits

This small cot blanket is a great introduction to quilting with free-hand embroidery. If you would like to learn how to draw with your sewing machine, Poppy Treffry's *Freehand Machine Embroidery*, in which this charming little project features, will provide you with a great introduction to this quick and easy technique.

AUGUST						
M	T	W	T	F	S	S
				1	2	3
4	5	6	7	8	9	10
11	12	13	14	15	16	17
18	19	20	21	22	23	24
25	26	27	28	29	30	31

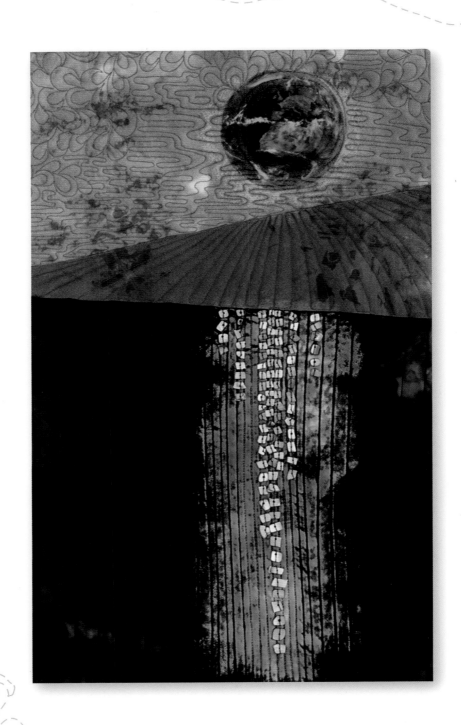

11
Monday

12
Tuesday

13
Wednesday

14
Thursday

15
Friday

16
Saturday

17
Sunday

			AUGUST			
M	T	W	T	F	S	S
				1	2	3
4	5	6	7	8	9	10
11	12	13	14	15	16	17
18	19	20	21	22	23	24
25	26	27	28	29	30	31

Moon's Reflection

This is one of four landscape-inspired hangings by Linda and Laura Kemshall developed to explore different painting techniques in their book *The Painted Quilt*. Shiny, tiny natural shell buttons have been used to create the moon's reflection.

18
Monday

19
Tuesday

20
Wednesday

21
Thursday

22
Friday

23
Saturday

24
Sunday

Pick and Mix

There is no better reason for making a quilt than falling in love with a fabric pack. When Angela Davies saw this Jelly Roll™ of 1930s reproduction fabrics at a quilt show, she couldn't wait to get started. The finished quilt was selected by Pam and Nicky Lintott to appear in *Jelly Roll Inspirations* along with the other winning designs of the 2009 Jelly Roll Challenge competition.

			AUGUST			
M	T	W	T	F	S	S
				1	2	3
4	5	6	7	8	9	10
11	12	13	14	15	16	17
18	19	20	21	22	23	24
25	26	27	28	29	30	31

August

25
Monday

26
Tuesday

27
Wednesday

28
Thursday

29
Friday

30
Saturday

31
Sunday

Butterfly, Butterfly

There are a total of 56 appliqué butterflies in this double-bed size quilt which features in Lynne Edwards' *Blanket Stitch Quilts*. Lynne's design was inspired by a pieced butterfly design seen on an antique quilt which she adapted to the stick-and-stitch appliqué technique. The butterfly block could be used in smaller projects too – you could make a cushion from one block or a cot quilt using 12.

AUGUST

M	T	W	T	F	S	S
				1	2	3
4	5	6	7	8	9	10
11	12	13	14	15	16	17
18	19	20	21	22	23	24
25	26	27	28	29	30	31

September

Labor Day (US)

1
Monday

2
Tuesday

3
Wednesday

4
Thursday

5
Friday

6
Saturday

Father's Day (Aus)

7
Sunday

Back to School

Quilt blocks representing well-known objects in pictorial form, such as houses, boats, baskets, flowers and trees, have long been popular in patchwork, and this charming quilt is a good example. One of 12 Jelly Roll™ designs featured in Pam and Nicky Lintott's *Antique to Heirloom Jelly Roll Quilts*, it features the very popular Schoolhouse block in soft, mellow colours.

SEPTEMBER

M	T	W	T	F	S	S
1	2	3	4	5	6	7
8	9	10	11	12	13	14
15	16	17	18	19	20	21
22	23	24	25	26	27	28
29	30					

September

8
Monday

9
Tuesday

10
Wednesday

11
Thursday

12
Friday

13
Saturday

14
Sunday

Birdhouse Bag

Australian-based designer Lynette Anderson grew up in an English country village and she has drawn on her childhood memories to create the cottage-garden inspired designs in *Country Cottage Quilting*. The birdhouse bag makes the perfect accompaniment to all those autumn craft shows – it is roomy, lightweight and has plenty of useful pockets.

			SEPTEMBER			
M	T	W	T	F	S	S
1	2	3	4	5	6	7
8	9	10	11	12	13	14
15	16	17	18	19	20	21
22	23	24	25	26	27	28
29	30					

September

15
Monday

16
Tuesday

17
Wednesday

18
Thursday

19
Friday

20
Saturday

21
Sunday

Sunset at Sisters
The Friendship Star is a traditional design often chosen by members of quilting groups to make quilts to welcome new members. Christine Porter designed this one to remind her of the happy times she spent teaching at the outdoor quilt show in Sisters, Oregon, and it is featured in her book *Tessellation Quilts*.

SEPTEMBER

M	T	W	T	F	S	S
1	2	3	4	5	6	7
8	9	10	11	12	13	14
15	16	17	18	19	20	21
22	23	24	25	26	27	28
29	30					

September

22
Monday

23
Tuesday

24
Wednesday

25
Thursday

26
Friday

27
Saturday

28
Sunday

Triangle Dynamics

In *Scrap Quilt Sensation* Katharine Guerrier showcases colourful quilt designs made from fabric leftovers and her vibrant designs are a great way to make a dent in your fabric stash. This quilt, for example, can be made any size divisible by the 30cm (12in) square blocks and, incredibly, it uses just a half-square triangle as its basic pieced unit.

		SEPTEMBER				
M	T	W	T	F	S	S
1	2	3	4	5	6	7
8	9	10	11	12	13	14
15	16	17	18	19	20	21
22	23	24	25	26	27	28
29	30					

September/October

29
Monday

30
Tuesday

1
Wednesday

2
Thursday

3
Friday

4
Saturday

5
Sunday

		OCTOBER				
M	T	W	T	F	S	S
		1	2	3	4	5
6	7	8	9	10	11	12
13	14	15	16	17	18	19
20	21	22	23	24	25	26
27	28	29	30	31		

Hometown
Susan Briscoe's *kunimoto* (hometown) quilt was made entirely from silk kimono fabrics and the circle appliqués are perfect for featuring the landscape scenes. Susan's book *Japanese Quilt Inspirations* is full of clever ideas for getting the most from Japanese fabrics.

October

6
Monday

7
Tuesday

8
Wednesday

9
Thursday

10
Friday

11
Saturday

12
Sunday

Framed by Diamonds

This design by Jill Randel was one of the winning entries in the Jelly Roll Dream Challenge. Jill was inspired by her love of Irish Chain quilts. You too can replicate her design using just one Jelly Roll™, but you'll need to make sure it has 10 strips in a distinctive colour to create the striking diamond design. All 12 prize-winning quilts can be seen in *Jelly Roll Dreams* compiled by Pam and Nicky Lintott.

OCTOBER

M	T	W	T	F	S	S
		1	2	3	4	5
6	7	8	9	10	11	12
13	14	15	16	17	18	19
20	21	22	23	24	25	26
27	28	29	30	31		

October

Columbus Day (US)

13
Monday

14
Tuesday

15
Wednesday

16
Thursday

17
Friday

18
Saturday

19
Sunday

Sashiko Settings

The Quilter's Bible by Linda Clements is full of clever techniques for combining patchwork, appliqué and quilting to create striking designs. A selection of specially-designed projects, including these stylish placemats made using sashiko machine quilting, gives plenty of opportunities to explore newly-discovered skills.

OCTOBER

M	T	W	T	F	S	S
		1	2	3	4	5
6	7	8	9	10	11	12
13	14	15	16	17	18	19
20	21	22	23	24	25	26
27	28	29	30	31		

20
Monday

21
Tuesday

22
Wednesday

23
Thursday

24
Friday

25
Saturday

26
Sunday

Hidden Treasure

Pam and Nicky Lintott's book *More Layer Cake, Jelly Roll & Charm Quilts* has all the help you need to get the most from your favourite pre-cut fabric bundles. This quilt, for example, is made from four charm packs used together with a neutral marble fabric, and a simple Nine-Patch block is transformed into a stunning design.

OCTOBER						
M	T	W	T	F	S	S
		1	2	3	4	5
6	7	8	9	10	11	12
13	14	15	16	17	18	19
20	21	22	23	24	25	26
27	28	29	30	31		

October/November

27
Monday

28
Tuesday

29
Wednesday

30
Thursday

Halloween

31
Friday

1
Saturday

2
Sunday

Twisting the Night Away

This quilt is an effective combination of two blocks – the Snowball and the Twist – and it is a great design for using large, bold floral prints. This is just one of 17 stunning designs featured in *Layer Cake, Jelly Roll and Charm Quilts* by Pam and Nicky Lintott, a book that is dedicated to providing ingenious ideas for using pre-cut fabric collections with little or no waste.

			OCTOBER			
M	T	W	T	F	S	S
		1	2	3	4	5
6	7	8	9	10	11	12
13	14	15	16	17	18	19
20	21	22	23	24	25	26
27	28	29	30	31		

November

3
Monday

4
Tuesday

5
Wednesday

6
Thursday

7
Friday

8
Saturday

9
Sunday

Cropped Pinwheels

Based on traditional Pinwheel blocks made from half-square triangle units, each block in this quilt is trimmed differently so that no two are the same. This is one of 12 beautiful scrap quilt designs featured in *Scrap Quilt Sensation* by Katharine Guerrier — a designer renowned for her expert handling of colour and her contemporary twist on traditional designs.

NOVEMBER

M	T	W	T	F	S	S
					1	2
3	4	5	6	7	8	9
10	11	12	13	14	15	16
17	18	19	20	21	22	23
24	25	26	27	28	29	30

November

10
Monday

Veterans Day (US)

11
Tuesday

12
Wednesday

13
Thursday

14
Friday

15
Saturday

16
Sunday

Razzle Dazzle

Pam and Nicky Lintott have an excellent reputation for creating quick and clever quilt designs from pre-cut fabric collections with little or no waste. This intricate-looking design from *Layer Cake, Jelly Roll and Charm Quilts* combines two similar patchwork blocks that look great when alternated – and best of all, it can be made from just one Jelly Roll™.

NOVEMBER						
M	T	W	T	F	S	S
					1	2
3	4	5	6	7	8	9
10	11	12	13	14	15	16
17	18	19	20	21	22	23
24	25	26	27	28	29	30

17
Monday

18
Tuesday

19
Wednesday

20
Thursday

21
Friday

22
Saturday

23
Sunday

Diamonds Are a Girl's Best Friend

Tina Kirschling's quilt is a delight for star quilt lovers with its
different size stars pieced cleverly together. Pam and Nicky Lintott
chose it as one of the winning entries in their Jelly Roll Dream
Challenge, published in their book *Jelly Roll Dreams*. When Tina
started quilting it was love at first stitch and she continues to enjoy
discovering new design possibilities with this rewarding hobby.

			NOVEMBER			
M	T	W	T	F	S	S
					1	2
3	4	5	6	7	8	9
10	11	12	13	14	15	16
17	18	19	20	21	22	23
24	25	26	27	28	29	30

November

24
Monday

25
Tuesday

26
Wednesday

Thanksgiving (US)

27
Thursday

28
Friday

29
Saturday

30
Sunday

Sweet Sixteen
This charming quilt has 16-patch blocks made up of 16 small squares of different fabrics. It is based on a classic American scrap quilt from the Great Depression, and Pam and Nicky Lintott's interpretation of this vintage design, which features in their book *Antique to Heirloom Jelly Roll Quilts*, uses just one Jelly Roll™.

NOVEMBER						
M	T	W	T	F	S	S
					1	2
3	4	5	6	7	8	9
10	11	12	13	14	15	16
17	18	19	20	21	22	23
24	25	26	27	28	29	30

December

1 Monday	
2 Tuesday	
3 Wednesday	
4 Thursday	
5 Friday	
6 Saturday	
7 Sunday	

Jelly Roll Sampler

There are just a few short weeks left to make that heirloom quilt you promised yourself at the beginning of the year, but fear not – there's still time yet. Pam and Nicky Lintott's *Jelly Roll Sampler Quilts* features a quick-to-piece classic sampler that can be made using just one Jelly Roll™.

DECEMBER

M	T	W	T	F	S	S
1	2	3	4	5	6	7
8	9	10	11	12	13	14
15	16	17	18	19	20	21
22	23	24	25	26	27	28
29	30	31				

December

8
Monday

9
Tuesday

10
Wednesday

11
Thursday

12
Friday

13
Saturday

14
Sunday

Christmas Gifts

At Christmas-time make the receiving of gifts extra special by presenting them in a handmade gift bag. Made from wool felt with a simple pieced border, charming festive motifs are appliquéd in the front panel and embellished with sparkling stitches. Barri Sue Gaudet of Bareroots has lots more quilted gift ideas for your family and friends in her book *Quilt a Gift*.

		DECEMBER				
M	T	W	T	F	S	S
1	2	3	4	5	6	7
8	9	10	11	12	13	14
15	16	17	18	19	20	21
22	23	24	25	26	27	28
29	30	31				

December

15
Monday

16
Tuesday

17
Wednesday

18
Thursday

19
Friday

20
Saturday

21
Sunday

Snowflake Rose

The quilt designs of Joanna Figueroa – founder of Fig Tree & Co and publisher of over 100 patterns – have a soft, vintage look about them, updated with clean, fresh colours. The fabric snowflakes on this quilt were pieced using simple and traditional strip piecing techniques using her Gypsy Rose fabric collection. Joanna shares her top tips for fabric and colour selection in *The Quiltmakers*.

DECEMBER

M	T	W	T	F	S	S
1	2	3	4	5	6	7
8	9	10	11	12	13	14
15	16	17	18	19	20	21
22	23	24	25	26	27	28
29	30	31				

December

22
Monday

23
Tuesday

24
Wednesday

Christmas Day

25
Thursday

Boxing Day (UK, Aus)

26
Friday

27
Saturday

28
Sunday

Christmas Night

The wait is nearly over and Christmas is almost here. This festive lap quilt is perfect for keeping you cosy at this special time of year. *Quilt a Gift for Christmas* by Barri Sue Gaudet of Bareroots is full of gorgeous projects to quilt and stitch to delight your family and friends, including quick and easy gift ideas.

			DECEMBER			
M	T	W	T	F	S	S
1	2	3	4	5	6	7
8	9	10	11	12	13	14
15	16	17	18	19	20	21
22	23	24	25	26	27	28
29	30	31				

29
Monday

30
Tuesday

31
Wednesday

New Year's Day

1
Thursday

2
Friday

3
Saturday

4
Sunday

Starry, Starry Night

This tessellating quilt from Christine Porter's *Tessellation Quilts* is made from her large collection of blue striped and checked fabrics. Each triangular unit has a pale central triangle and is surrounded with dark or medium blue strips, each of which has a yellow diamond on one end. When the resulting larger triangle units are joined in rows, six pointed stars appear at the intersections.

JANUARY 2015						
M	T	W	T	F	S	S
			1	2	3	4
5	6	7	8	9	10	11
12	13	14	15	16	17	18
19	20	21	22	23	24	25
26	27	28	29	30	31	

Useful Information

It is hoped that the quilt photographs featured in this diary have inspired you to take your own quilt skills further. Wherever you are located, there are bound to be opportunities for you to see other quilters' work and to share your love of this amazing textile art. Use the following information to help you find out what is going on near you.

UK
Organizations

The Quilters' Guild of the British Isles is an independent registered educational charity with over 7,000 members. www.quiltersguild.org.uk

Exhibitions

The Festival of Quilts
Organized by Creative Exhibitions Ltd with the support of the Quilters Guild of the British Isles, this is the largest quilt show in Europe with over 30,000 visitors each year. A four-day show held in August at the National Exhibition Centre, Birmingham, it has over 1,000 competition quilts on display, as well as galleries from leading international quilt artists and groups. There are over 300 exhibitors selling specialist patchwork and quilting supplies, plus hundreds of masterclasses, workshops and lectures.
www.twistedthread.com

Quilts UK
The organizers of this exhibition, Grosvenor Shows Ltd, hold several patchwork and quilting exhibitions nationally each year. The largest of these is Quilts UK held in May at the Three Counties Showground in the beautiful Malvern Hills in Worcestershire. The longest established show in the UK, it attracts over 9,000 visitors annually. It is an open competitive show with over 400 quilts on display and 150 trade stands.
www.grosvenorexhibitions.co.uk

The National Quilt Championships
An open competitive quilt show held at Sandown Park in June attracting over 5,000 visitors. Over 400 quilts are on display, including features from well-known artists from the UK and overseas, incorporating a mix of traditional and contemporary quilts.
www.grosvenorexhibitions.co.uk

Spring and Autumn Quilt Festivals
A number of smaller, local quilt shows are also organized by Grosvenor Shows Ltd. Locations include: Ardingly, Duxford, Edinburgh, Exeter, Maidstone and Malvern.
www.grosvenorexhibitions.co.uk

Quiltfest
Quiltfest's aim is to showcase the cutting edge of textile design and making, and to enable quiltmakers in Wales and the Northwest of England to see work that may not normally be exhibited in the region. It is an annual show held in February at Llangollen Museum and Art Gallery.
www.quiltfest.org.uk

USA
Organizations

American Quilter's Society (AQS)
The aim of the AQS is to provide a forum for quilters of all skill levels to expand their horizons in quiltmaking, design, self-expression and quilt collecting. It publishes books and magazines, has product offers, and runs quilt shows and contests, workshops and other activities.
www.americanquilter.com

The International Quilting Association (IQA)
The IQA is a non-profit organization dedicated to the preservation of the art of quilting, the attainment of public recognition for quilting as an art form, and the advancement of the state of the art throughout the world. Founded in 1979, it supports many quilting projects and activities, and organizes two annual Judged Shows of members' work exhibited at the International Quilt Markets and Festivals held throughout the year.
www.quilts.com

Exhibitions

American Quilter's Society Quilt Shows
The AQS organizes a number of quilt shows annually and in 2014 these will be held in Paducah, Kentucky (April), Grand Rapids, Michigan (August), and Des Moines, Iowa (October).
www.americanquilter.com

The International Quilting Association Quilt Shows
Quilts, Inc., the IQA's exhibiton arm, holds three consumer shows (Quilt Festival) and two trade shows (Quilt Market) annually.
www.quilts.com

Sisters Outdoor Quilt Show
This is the largest outdoor quilt show in the world with over 12,500 attendees and is held on the second Saturday of July in Sisters, Oregon.
www.sistersoutdoorquiltshow.org

The Mancuso Quilt Shows
Mancuso Show Management, run by brothers David and Peter Mancuso, promotes seven major national and international quilting and textile arts festivals held across the USA.
www.quiltfest.com

CANADA
Organizations

Canadian Quilters' Association
Formed in 1981, the aims and objectives of the Canadian Quilters' Association are: to promote a greater understanding, appreciation, and knowledge of the art, techniques, and heritage of patchwork, appliqué, and quilting; to promote the highest standards of workmanship and design in both traditional and innovative work; and to foster cooperation and sharing among quiltmakers. There are a number of Canadian Quilters' Association sponsored events including the National Juried Show (NJS), Canada's most prestigious quilt show.
www.canadianquilter.com

AUSTRALIA
Organizations

The Quilters' Guild of NSW
A Sydney-based organization which aims to promote the art and craft of patchwork and quilting. Membership is open to anyone with an interest in the craft, from the beginner to the professional, and it has over 1,000 members.
www.quiltersguildnsw.com

Quilters' Guild of South Australia
This organization has over 500 individual guild members with over 100 city and country groups now affiliated with the guild.
www.saquilters.org.au

Exhibitions

Australia's No.1 Craft and Quilt Fairs
Expertise Events run several craft and quilting fairs in Australia (Perth, Sydney, Launceston – Tasmania, Melbourne, Canberra, Brisbane, Adelaide) and New Zealand (Hamilton).
www.craftfair.com.au

The Australasian Quilt Convention (AQC)
Held in Melbourne, this is Australia's largest annual quilt-dedicated event, incorporating classes and lectures with highly skilled tutors, much-anticipated social events, a shopping market plus exhibitor workshops and exclusive quilt displays. It brings together thousands of quilters from all over Australia and around the world.
www.aqc.com.au

NEW ZEALAND
Organizations

Aotearoa National Association of New Zealand Quilters
Formed in 1994 as the National Association of New Zealand Quilters (NANZQ) the principle objective is to promote and lead the development of patchwork, quilting and textile artists within New Zealand.
www.aotearoaquilters.co.nz

More About the Quilts

The quilts included in the *Quilter's Desk Diary 2014* have all been selected from the great range of patchwork and quilting books published by David & Charles. If you would like to find out more about any of the quilt designs featured, why not treat yourself to a few of these great books. For more information about these and other high quality craft books visit: **www.stitchcraftcreate.co.uk**

Antique to Heirloom Jelly Roll Quilts
Pam & Nicky Lintott

ISBN-13: 978-1-4463-0182-1

Twelve new Jelly Roll™ quilt designs based on the best antique quilts from Pam Lintott's stunning vintage collection. Each clever quilt pattern uses just one Jelly Roll™.

Beginner's Guide to Quilting
Elizabeth Betts

ISBN-13: 978-1-4463-0254-5

Learn all the quilting basics, from paper piecing to appliqué to hand and machine quilting. Features 16 simple projects, from bags and cushions to wall hangings and quilts.

Blanket Stitch Quilts
Lynne Edwards

ISBN-13: 978-1-4463-0136-4

Learn to sew beautiful handmade quilts with simple blanket stitch appliqué technique. Choose from 12 inspiring projects.

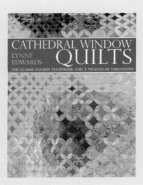

Cathedral Window Quilts
Lynne Edwards

ISBN-13: 978-0-7153-2713-5

Explore classic techniques using fabulous fabrics to create over 25 flamboyantly folded projects, ranging from heirloom quilts and striking wall hangings to colourful, quick-to-make cushions, bags and pincushions.

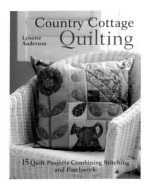

Country Cottage Quilting
Lynette Anderson

ISBN-13: 978-1-4463-0039-8

The country cottage garden provides the inspiration for this collection of beautiful quilting and stitchery designs, featuring wall quilts, bags, cushion covers, all in Lynette's distinctive style.

Cushions & Quilts
Jo Colwill

ISBN-13: 978-1-4463-0256-9

A collection of 20 projects for a range of cushions and quilts, all inspired by Jo Colwill's life on her Cornish farm. Includes Jo's trademark cushion styles and features all her quilting and sewing tips and advice.

Features a full sized pattern for the Advent Calender Quilt.

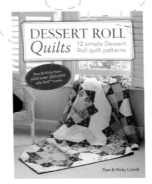

Dessert Roll Quilts
Pam & Nicky Lintott

ISBN-13: 978-1-4463-0354-2

Twelve quilt patterns provide inspiration for beginners and experienced quilters too for using the latest Dessert Roll™ pre-cut fabrics from Moda.

Easy Japanese Quilt Style
Julia Davis & Anne Muxworthy

ISBN-13: 978-0-7153-2862-0

The perfect book for quilters of all abilities who want to introduce Japanese style into their homes with ingenious quick-to-stitch projects, ranging from bags to wall hangings.

The Essential Sampler Quilt Book
Lynne Edwards

ISBN-13: 978-0-7153-3613-7

Masterclass instruction from the sampler quilt expert for making 40 pieced blocks using both hand and machine techniques, with a wealth of quilt photographs to inspire colour and fabric choices.

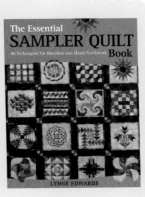

Folk Quilt Appliqué
Clare Kingslake

ISBN-13: 978-0-7153-3826-1

Drawing on a palette of soft, country colours, Clare Kingslake presents a collection of 20 irresistible projects in a her quirky folk style, using both hand and machine appliqué techniques.

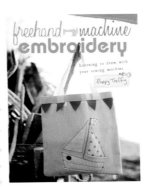

Freehand Machine Embroidery
Poppy Treffry

ISBN-13: 978-1-4463-0186-9

Get creative with your sewing machine and learn the secrets of freehand machine embroidery while making fun and original gifts for family and friends.

Japanese Quilt Inspirations
Susan Briscoe

ISBN-13: 978-0-7153-3827-8

Ten stunning quilt designs that make clever use of fabric favourites such as fat quarters, strip rolls and feature panels, as well as kimono widths and furoshiki (wrapping cloths).

Japanese Sashiko Inspirations
Susan Briscoe

ISBN-13: 978-0-7153-2641-4

Discover sashiko, the Japanese method of decorative stitching to create striking patterns on fabric with lines of simple running stitch. Bring a touch of the Orient to your home with over 25 projects to choose from.

Jelly Roll Dreams
Pam & Nicky Lintott

ISBN-13: 978-1-4463-0040-4

A stunning showcase for the 12 winning quilts from the 2011 Jelly Roll Dream Challenge, each made from just one Jelly Roll™, with variations provided by Pam & Nicky Lintott.

Jelly Roll Inspirations
Pam & Nicky Lintott

ISBN-13: 978-0-7153-3311-2

The aim of the Jelly Roll Challenge competition was to find the best and most creative use of just one jelly roll. Gathered here are the 12 fabulous winning entries, with step-by-step instructions and a colour variation on each.

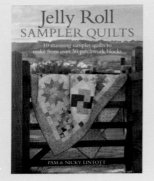

Jelly Roll Sampler Quilts
Pam & Nicky Lintott

ISBN-13: 978-0-7153-3844-5

Making a sampler quilt featuring as many different patchwork blocks as possible is every quilter's dream. All you jelly roll lovers out there, make the dream come true.

Layer Cake, Jelly Roll and Charm Quilts
Pam & Nicky Lintott

ISBN-13: 978-0-7153-3208-5

Seventeen beautiful projects, from lap quilts to bed quilts, show you how to get the most from irresistible pre-cut fabric bundles.

Making Welsh Quilts
Mary Jenkins &
Clare Claridge

ISBN-13: 978-0-7153-2996-2

This book explores the fascinating history of Welsh quilting and features 10 sumptuous projects for you to make in the traditional style, using strikingly simple patchwork designs and decorative quilting patterns.

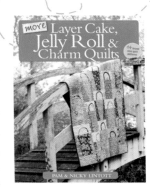

More Layer Cake, Jelly Roll & Charm Quilts
Pam & Nicky Lintott

ISBN-13: 978-0-7153-3898-8

A second helping of 14 brand new quilt designs to help quilters get the most from favourite pre-cut fabric bundles, for quilts that are quick to piece and a joy to make.

The Painted Quilt
Linda & Laura Kemshall

ISBN-13: 978-0-7153-2450-9

This inspirational book demystifies the process of colouring cloth by various means including fabric paints, pastels, dyes, bleaches and transfers. Simple techniques are combined to produce complex textile surfaces, all easily explained step by step.

Pretty Patchwork Gifts
Helen Philipps

ISBN-13: 978-1-4463-0213-2

Over 25 simple sewing projects that combine patchwork, appliqué and embroidery, from corsages and purses to bags and cushions.

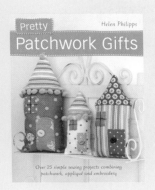

Quilt a Gift
Barri Sue Gaudet

ISBN-13: 978-0-7153-3282-5

Whether you have a week, a day, or just a couple of hours to stitch it, you'll find the perfect gift idea here for family or friends, whatever the occasion.

Quilt a Gift for Christmas
Barri Sue Gaudet

ISBN-13: 978-1-4463-0184-5

Whether you have a week, a day, or just a couple of hours, you can stitch, sew and quilt gorgeous Christmas projects for all your family and friends.

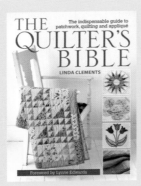

The Quilter's Bible
Lin Clements

ISBN-13: 978-0-7153-3626-7

This is the ultimate quilter's companion to over 220 patchwork, quilting and appliqué techniques, and it is illustrated with more than 800 colour diagrams.

The Quilters' Guild Collection
Editor: Bridget Long

ISBN-13: 978-0-7153-2668-8

The Quilters' Guild Heritage Collection is the largest collection of patchwork and quilting in the UK, dating back as far as the 18th century. Twelve contemporary quiltmakers each take inspiration from a heritage piece to make a project for today.

The Quiltmakers
Consultant Editor: Pam Lintott

ISBN-13: 978-0-7153-3173-6

A unique opportunity to take eight masterclasses from some of the very best quilters in the world, without ever leaving home. Topics include creating perspective, perfect piecing, and inspired fabric collage.

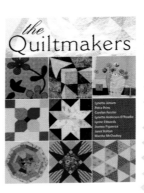

Scrap Quilt Sensation
Katharine Guerrier

ISBN-13: 978-0-7153-2452-3

A sumptuous collection of scrap quilts with a contemporary twist on traditional designs. Twelve step-by-step projects, with in-depth advice on selecting the right fabrics from your stash and how to combine them for best effect.

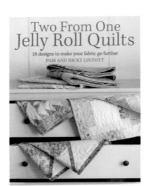

Tessellation Quilts
Christine Porter

ISBN-13: 978-0-7153-1941-3

Discover how you can translate simple interlocking patterns into stunning pieced patchwork designs. Nine tessellating block designs are explored in detail, with over 45 quilts illustrating how the blocks can be used in very different ways.

Two from One Jelly Roll Quilts
Pam & Nicky Lintott

ISBN-13: 978-0-7153-3756-1

Learn how to make two different quilts using just one jelly roll – half the fabric, twice the inspiration. It features 18 patterns to help you make your fabric go further.

More About the Quiltmakers

The quilt designs featured in *The Quilter's Desk Diary 2014* showcase the talents of some of the world's most respected and creative quiltmakers. The names of those whose work is included are listed below.

Mary Claire Allen, **Tina Kirschling**, **Jill Randel** and **Brenda Sander** were all finalists in the 2011 Jelly Roll Dream Challenge.

Lynette Anderson was born in Dorset, England and moved to Australia in 1990 where she founded The Patchwork Angel store in 1997. Lynette is now focussed full time on designing her extensive pattern range, as well as fabrics for Henry Glass & Co.
www.lynetteandersondesigns.typepad.com

Elizabeth Betts runs her Brighton-based quilting shop, Quilty Pleasures, with her mother Susan. *Beginner's Guide to Quilting* is her first book.
www.quilty-pleasures.co.uk

Susan Briscoe was introduced to sashiko while teaching English in Japan. Susan's sashiko designs have been published in *Popular Patchwork*, *British Patchwork & Quilting* and *Fabrications*, and she has written over ten books on quilting.
www.susanbriscoe.co.uk

Clare Claridge is a world expert on Welsh quilting patterns, and she is the co-author of *Making Welsh Quilts*.

Linda Clements has been a specialist craft editor for many years and is author of the best-selling *The Quilter's Bible*. Passionate about quilting, she has learnt and developed her skills by working with some of the best quilting teachers.

Jo Colwill runs her shop and workshop space – Cowslip Workshops – from her organic farm in Launceston, Cornwall. She has been quilting and teaching for over 20 years and is highly respected in the quilting community.
www.cowslipworkshops.co.uk

Angela Davies was one of the finalists in the 2009 Jelly Roll Challenge.

Julia Davis and **Anne Muxworthy** run the Step By Step Patchwork Centre in South Molton, Devon. They specialize in Japanese fabrics, and offer several kits that make great use of them.
www.stepbystep-quilts.co.uk

Lynne Edwards specializes in sampler quilts and the cathedral window technique. She has been the recipient of many prestigious awards including the Jewel Pearce Patterson Scholarship for International Quilt Teachers and the Amy Emms Memorial Trophy. In 2008 she was awarded an MBE for services to Arts and Crafts.

Joanna Figueroa is a talented designer and quiltmaker and founder of Fig Tree & Co. Joanna designs the gorgeous Fig Tree fabrics for Moda fabrics. She has published over 100 quilting, sewing and children's patterns and design booklets.
www.figtreeandco.com

Barri Sue Gaudet runs her own pattern company, Bareroots. She travels widely to teach, and also runs a stitchery and knitting shop in Bishop, California named Sierra Cottons & Wools.
www.bareroots.com

Katharine Guerrier is the author of numerous books and she contributes regularly to several quilting magazines with articles, projects and reviews.
www.katharineguerrier.com

Mary Jenkins is a collector of Welsh quilts and samplers. An experienced author, she has written several books including co-authoring *Making Welsh Quilts*. Mary lives in Cardiff, Wales.
littlewelshquiltsandothertraditions.blogspot.co.uk

Clare Kingslake is an expert in appliqué techniques. Her popular designs have been featured in magazines in the UK and France.
www.clarespatterns.co.uk

Laura Kemshall and **Linda Kemshall** are renowned for their innovative approach to textiles as well as their City & Guilds creative courses through their fully accredited online centre. Laura also designs and produces an exclusive range of products available through her online DesignMatters Store.
www.lindakemshall.com

Pam Lintott and **Nicky Lintott** run The Quilt Room in Dorking, Surrey. Pam's first book, *The Quilt Room*, was a compilation of work from the very best patchworkers. Pam has also written several books with daughter Nicky, whose main focus is on developing their longarm quilting business.
www.quiltroom.co.uk

Marsha McCloskey specializes in Feathered Star designs. She has written and co-authored over 25 books on quiltmaking, including *Marsha McCloskey's Block Party*. She runs Feathered Star Productions, Inc., an online resource.
www.marshamccloskey.com

Helen Philipps studied printed textiles and embroidery at Manchester Metropolitan University before becoming a freelance designer. Her work regularly features in popular craft magazines.
www.helenphilipps.blogspot.co.uk

Christine Porter teaches, lectures and judges in the US, Canada, Europe and the Middle East. She is also the British coordinator for the World Quilt and Textile competition.
www.christineporterquilts.com

Poppy Treffry runs a busy textile design company based in Cornwall. Her range of quirky accessories for fashion and the home sells in department stores and boutiques throughout the UK, USA, Japan and Europe.
www.poppytreffry.co.uk

A DAVID & CHARLES BOOK
© F&W Media International, Ltd 2013

David & Charles is an imprint of F&W Media International, Ltd
Brunel House, Forde Close, Newton Abbot, TQ12 4PU, UK

F&W Media International, Ltd is a subsidiary of F+W Media, Inc
10151 Carver Road, Suite #200 Blue Ash, OH 45242, USA

Text, layout and photography © F&W Media International, Ltd 2013

First published in the UK and USA in 2013

A catalogue record for this book is available from the British Library.

ISBN-13: 978-1-4463-0323-8 hardback
ISBN-10: 1-4463-0323-3 hardback

Printed in China by Toppan Leefung Printing Limited for:
F&W Media International, Ltd
Brunel House, Forde Close, Newton Abbot, TQ12 4PU, UK

Front cover quilt designed by Tina Kirschling, photographed by Lorna Yabsley for *Jelly Roll Dreams* (Pam & Nicky Lintott, 2012).

Back cover quilt designed by Katharine Guerrier, photographed by Kim Sayer for *Scrap Quilt Sensation* (Katharine Guerrier, 2007).

F+W Media publishes high quality books on a wide range of subjects. For more great book ideas visit: **www.stitchcraftcreate.co.uk**